NLP Neuro Linguistic Programming for Beginners

Transform Your Life Using NLP Hypnosis

By Hannah Zachary

Contents

Introduction to NLP

Neuro-linguistic programming, shortened to NLP, is a learning system that develops language through making connections between various senses.

Primarily, it is used to train new habits, alter perceptions of past experiences, and mentally formulating scenarios through which one can gain a new perspective on the world around them to develop those new behaviors and habits.

In some cases, this procedure can be crucial to recovering from mental illness. In others, it's just another way to better one's life.

Compared to other, solely physical approaches, neuro-linguistic programming is much more specialized.

Because it relies on reproducing talents on both a mental and physical level to learn them, it offers the greatest improvement in its users as compared to those other methods. Practicing it also leads to improvement in self-motivation and responsibility.

Furthermore, NLP leads users beyond the threshold that allows them to further amplify their mental and physical talents.

All of these phenomena work together to boost self-confidence and the drive to pursue life goals.

NLP pertains to neurological and linguistic factors in individuals as those areas are crucial to encountering essential human experiences. Subsets of these areas are the formulation of planned thoughts and biopsychological events through which thoughts are produced.

It helps us to overcome the barriers of pretense, assumptions, and stereotypes as well as developing a system of understanding for a sense of community and who the community itself functions on both large and small scales.

NLP can also foster self-discovery through introspection that allows you to properly gauge where you are in your life and which directions are right for you.

Doubts frequently arise when it's time to choose a career; in those cases, NLP can make a big difference on your outlook on your options.

If you can discover what truly drives you, there will be no doubts as to what you should do with your life. However, keep in mind that if you are in a dire situation, moving towards your dream job may not always be the best option. Settle for something else until you have everything in place to succeed.

Learning NLP leads to easier completion of long-term goals, but the best way to use it is to accomplish many small goals that are parts of larger objectives.

All that NLP requires of you is that you are determined, willing to acquire necessary skills, and have the motivation to push through hardships. Once the process starts, it can only build upon itself, and you'll find that your momentum is becoming unstoppable somewhere down the road.

You've probably been told – or at least heard – to be a leader, not a follower. In this situation, that might not necessarily be true. In fact, it's the opposite. There are many things worth following: your dreams, your heart, and your passion. Keeping those three things ahead of you always is the key to success.

Remember to look at your future in terms of your happiness. Picture yourself as a typesetter when you've always wanted to be a mechanic. Aren't your bored? You should be. No job is worth it if it doesn't speak with your heart. Take responsibility in pursuing an occupation that suits you and don't stop moving towards that goal until every imaginable resource has been exhausted.

When people land jobs that they're typically not too fond of, they tend to stick around anyway. There are several reasons for this. The biggest is probably that there are important things in their life that motivate them to maintain.

These include providing money for a family, or saving up for a necessary investment. However, if an individual can effectively communicate with those meaningful people, they shouldn't have to bend themselves to the expectations and desires of others. Those people can be made to understand your passions and will allow you some freedom from their expectations to pursue your dreams.

It's not the only method by far, but NLP is definitely one of the most unique. If you've never heard of it, it may prove to be a fresh perspective in helping you to discover what of the many things the world has to offer brings you happiness.

If you can use NLP to help you overcome whatever shell you might be trapped in, then the possibilities will unravel before you. Without other people, not only would life be dull and boring, but you'd have no resources through which to advance.

That's why a practice based on linguistics and communication is so effective in helping anyone to achieve their goals.

NLPs Connection to Hypnosis

Hypnosis is a trance-like state during which one is susceptible to suggestion. Rather than catering to the conscious mind, it interacts with the subconscious one – the part of the mind believed to be primarily responsible for behaviors and habits.

Hypnotists and psychological therapists typically use hypnosis to discover underlying, repressed stimuli of more evident problems or to develop self-esteem, get rid of addictions, as well as train people to do things they would otherwise not do.

For instance, if you develop an addiction to smoking with the idea that you can't break free from it, then you might need hypnosis so that you can attempt to transform those negative thoughts into positive ones.

Believe it or not, hypnosis has been of use to a great many people, even those who find it hard to believe in practices that seem as supernatural as hypnosis. It just comes to prove that anything within reason in this world is possible so long as you're willing to put effort towards it.

Take note that hypnosis observed success doesn't make it the premiere go-to solution for those looking to build upon themselves. Its effectiveness typically depends on how open the patient is to the process, and such should mostly be looked at as a supplement to other processes.

When all is said and done, it fails to be a core aspect of augmenting your mental and behavioral habits.

If you remain interested in the prospect of hypnosis, there are several facts that you should commit to memory and use when reaching your ultimate conclusion.

They are as follows:

1.   Hypnosis can only effectively occur with the help of a trained professional (you cannot induce a state of hypnosis on yourself and give yourself cues and impressions). Some practitioners require a recommendation while some do not; some charge and others will be willing to practice for free. Research your options and select the venue that best accommodates your specific needs. Also know that in order for hypnosis to work, you may have to

share troubling information with your hypnotist so that they may have a solid understanding of your situation and how to alleviate your problems.

2. Whether or not hypnosis is real is an object of much debate. Many theories seek to legitimize the practice, citing the calm, objective state in which people are capable of making the best decisions. Others criticize the supernatural aspect of achieving complete change through submission to the will of others. The most widely recognized explanation of hypnosis states that words or ideas with strong ties to the patient can be used to coax them into either abandoning or strengthening their positive or negative connection with that word or idea.

3. Hypnosis is extensively used today in the treatment of many psychological issues, depression and drug addiction for instance. Most find it difficult, even impossible, to put an end to addiction without participating in rehabilitation programs. Hypnosis makes weaning off of addiction much simpler. Another use is

developing higher self-esteem or self-worth, which inevitably aids you in overcoming any other obstacles you may have. In short, it has succeeded in enough cases of goal-reaching and personality-building to be viewed as a viable medical technique.

Because of the mysticism and skepticism surrounding hypnosis, there are a great deal of scam artists out there who will take advantage of curiosity and misinformation to perform gimmick hypnotisms, and you may not know that you've been fooled until it's too late to get your money back and the practitioner is nowhere to be found.

Therefore, once you have decided that you're willing to go through with hypnotism, the first step is to commit yourself to extensive research on your nearby hypnotists.

Which ones have degrees in psychology and permits to practice? Without one or both of those things, you shouldn't expect much.

If you're one of those who doesn't believe in hypnotism, this option shouldn't be considered even as a last resort.

If you're already wired to believe that hypnotism is fake, even the best hypnotist will be able to do nothing for you. You must make the choice to submit yourself to them and open up to the possibilities you seek to unlock.

In some ways, the effect of hypnotism is much like that of a sick person who gets well because they believe they will as opposed to a sick person who dies because they have little faith in survival.

In essence, if your mind is deadest on believing that your body can't recover from an ailment, the chances of recovery are reduced. Real scientific study has linked a positive outlook on life to increased health.

Using NLP to Enhance Your Life

The Neuro-Linguistic Program is especially useful in helping people to develop the self-confidence they need to pursue life goals. The programming extensively involves communication through speech.

In terms of personality, temperance, attitude, intelligence, technical ability, and beliefs, every human is truly unique.

Some people love to be the center of attention while others prefer to retreat into the background. If they're satisfied with that life, there's nothing that can be done, but if they want to break free from that shell, NLP is a legitimate method.

Respect is never gained without the use of communication, and one can't survive without doing so. Everyone needs to be able to communicate what necessities they require as well as what things may be bringing them harm if they are to thrive. Communication with family and friends is typically simple. Strangers prove more difficult. In situations where one isn't comfortable, they experience difficulty in clearly expressing their harbored emotions.

In these cases, the least embarrassing or stressful course of action is to keep quiet, a habit that develops into a lack of confidence. NLP's focus on communication is what makes it such an effective resource in helping people to come to terms with their fears.

Sometimes, formulating ideas into words and words into conversations isn't the issue. Some people are excellent in developing these ideas in their minds, but suffer when it comes time to verbally express them.

Once the spotlight is directed on them, all those great ideas just seem to disappear and they're left clueless and puzzled, frantically searching for words with which to rebound. This is a different problem entirely.

NLP has a specific training regiment dedicated to this speech impediment, as well specific programs for nearly every problem it seeks to correct. Before beginning any type of conditioning, it is your responsibility to assess as precisely as possible what it is about yourself you seek to change.

Only after that should you consider looking for the right treatment.

If you're not strong of character, this is the appropriate time to build yourself up. Discipline and honesty are crucial to the success of the programming. If you can't draw an honest portrait of yourself, no amount of treatment will ever suffice in helping you to become the person you want to be.

Having a part of yourself that you aren't particularly proud off isn't an oddity at all. We all have quirks about us. However, if you feel crippled by it and want to make a change, but aren't willing to perhaps go out of your way to mold yourself into the person you want to be, you're doing yourself a great disservice. At the end of the day, you'll have locked yourself inside your own personal jail.

Obviously, jail in these sense doesn't refer to an institution for criminals, but rather a mindset where people are unwilling to explore themselves, understand themselves, and change themselves.

These people possess limiting beliefs that prevent them from moving forward out of ruts even if progression is all they've ever wanted.

The only way to escape from this jail is through acknowledging the problem and forcibly taking steps to diminish or eliminate it entirely. During this period, seek out NLP training to assist you.

Engage in conversations with others whenever you can; talking about yourself is one of the best ways to get to know yourself. You'd be surprised how much about yourself that you would have never believed if no one asked you about it. Use this opportunity to learn yourself and open up to the many possibilities surrounding you.

This largely contrasts what most people would say, which is that they know themselves completely, more than anyone else.

The truth is, sometimes others understand you better than you do because they observe what they see without having to be embarrassed or ashamed of those qualities. That aside, there's always more you can learn about yourself, so make an active effort to discover those things.

Engage in as many various activities as you can; experiment with many things that you don't think you'll have a taste for but have never tried.

People are complex; while certain personality types are more attuned to certain activities, there's no clear-cut way of determining what you will find pleasurable.

In today's society, more than ever, being able to effectively communicate leads to more opportunities. Even if you don't immediately start with face-to-face conversations, the new age has given us the gifts of email and texting.

You can work your way up gradually. When you're ready, start orally communicating your thoughts and feelings, first with people who you're most comfortable with.

When that becomes effortless, move on to friends who you aren't as well acquainted with as family. Gradually move down and down the ladder until you can effectively speak with total strangers.

Go ahead and break down NLP once more to find that it is somewhere within all of us.

Neuro for the biological mental processes, linguistic for the communication and speech aspects, and program for the process of reprogramming yourself in an ideal light.

Goals, tangible and intangible, grow ever closer through use of the neuro-linguistic program. If you're looking to make something of your life but don't know where to start, why not give it a try?

It may not work to your best expectations, but you won't have wasted your time because you'll have developed great skills that you can allocate towards different programs as you continue to grow.

As a stepping stone or long-term investment, NLP is a fantastic tool for the arduous journey of transforming yourself from ordinary into extraordinary.

NLP and Breaking Down Barriers

The principles of Neuro Linguistic programming can be used to break down barriers caused by the inability to properly communicate, both with yourself and with others

If the problem is communicating with yourself, it may take the form of mental barriers which can be quite troublesome to conquer. Some people have a general distaste for speaking and prefer to let others speak for them.

Obviously, that person's true nature can never be determined by third parties because they never get a first person experience.

If those people could muster the strength to speak for themselves, they'd be building skills to assist them for the rest of their lives.

Fear of Rejection

It is no mystery why people refuse to express themselves in given situations. Many people get nervous when they have to speak to crowds and no one wants to incriminate themselves by speaking out of line to a superior or to anyone with a hold over them. That fear of rejection occurs with everyone on a daily level.

Some of us, however, are more capable of overcoming it and don't notice it nearly as much. If one wants to succeed in defeating this fear, they must come to realize that everyone will not ever agree with anything you say.

Whenever you speak, you should expect someone in the room to have different feelings on the subject than you do. You also need to realize that your ideas may be flawed, and that might be a contributing factor to your rejection.

In this case, you can use criticisms to enhance the way you think and speak about the world around you.

Being able to critically analyze your own statements is a valuable ability in self-improvement; you may learn to reform your original idea into a concept that everyone can at least understand and sympathize with, even if they don't agree.

If you can take rejection in perspective, it can help you to think more abstractly to generate ideas that won't be rejected.

Fear of Failure

No one lives with the mindset that they want to fail in life. Nonetheless, reviewing the lives of some of the world's greatest people reveals that the accumulation of failures is a necessary step to gaining the courage and confidence required to stand down adversity.

Neuro Linguistic Programming examines people's mentalities and how they contribute to both failure and success. Those who build up from their failures tend to be successful while those who are torn down by failures tend to continue failing.

Coming Out of Your Shell

Out of unbearable shame or embarrassment, many people freeze up when required to speak in front of groups of people, even if the group is small. NLP is a great tool for helping you to vanquish that fear of public speaking.

Once you have come to grip the reality that there are areas in your life that could use improvement, you can move on to researching and consulting to discover the NLP plan that fits your specific needs. The only way to do this is to question yourself; maybe find a few online questionnaires. The more you know about yourself, the easier it will be to discern the proper course of action – not only that, but you will feel invigorated by coming to better understand who exactly you are. It's also vastly more efficient than shelling out your own cash in "self-discovery" programs.

That goes without saying that NLP may not be a completely free experience for you. There are instances where it can be absolutely necessary for you to make an investment of some sort (for example, if you decide that you need to see a professional psychiatric consultant).

But what's important here is that when compared to other options, NLP is pretty close to free! A lot of what you need to know about the process can be found for free all across the interwebs. You don't have to push yourself into poverty for the sake of becoming a better person.

On the contrary, you should be rewarded for it; and successful execution of NLP is certainly a reward in itself. If you have the courage to face your flaws and the determination to change them, neuro-linguistic programming will lead you down the most profitable path in life.

NLP and Prevailing over Procrastination

As we all likely know, procrastination is, to reference a common saying, putting off today what could be done tomorrow.

Essentially, it is tackling all of your problems at once as opposed to gradually completing them. If you want to use NLP to correct this habit, you must first ask yourself, "what is the cause of my procrastination?"

The reasons are as infinite as there are people, but the main ones are poor environments for task completion, personal or spiritual beliefs, and pure laziness. Some studies even indicated that those who are hassled tend to procrastinate more than those who are given their own time frame to work with.

What triggers procrastination?

• Stress. Stress can be attributed as a cause of nearly everything. If we have a heavy workload and that workload causes stress, we'll try to relieve the stress by putting off the work. Anxiety and fear can also be causes of stress and procrastination. Procrastination is used to cope with these trying situations. Your mind convinces your body that by foregoing the work, you will feel better. Unfortunately, it's only a temporary fix and increases stress that you'll experience in the future.

• Laziness. Consistent emotional and physical lassitude can also trigger procrastination. If a given task requires more energy than you're willing to exert at the moment, a lazy individual will simply decide not to participate, preferring smaller, simper tasks. The lazy person rationalizes that they have conserved energy, put as they continue to put off the task, it begins to require more and more energy to complete at the same level of quality as when first assigned. Lazy procrastinators don't realize that it would actually require less energy to complete the task when it first appears.

• Ineptitude. Of all the causes of stress, incompetence is the most difficult for people to admit to themselves. No one wants to be bad at things; people naturally strive to excel. An example is if you are given a task but are unsure if you can complete it. However, the task is mandatory, and you must try your hand at it.

The fear of producing a mediocre product causes you to procrastinate. If you never attempt it, you can't fail, right? If you make a habit out of it, procrastination due to ineptitude can be heavily crippling.

• Perfectionism. The opposite of ineptitude, perfectionism involves having the ability to perform exemplarily but not settling for anything less than the best. The individual may not put off the task, but they will work beyond deadlines to make the perfect product.

Regardless of why procrastination occurs, the solutions are generally the same. The first step in this process is defining a purpose for yourself, what you live for. Depending on the individual, you may need to muster some motivation.

Types of Motivation

Motivation can be crudely divided into two halves: fear-induced motivation and greed-induced motivation. It's not unusual for one person to experience both of these simultaneously, but they tend to lean towards one over the other.

This is an important aspect of NLP because of the human motivational orientation used in it. This is the process of changing what aspects of your life motivate you. When you want to overcome procrastination, it is essential that you find something that motivates you to complete whatever tasks you're reluctant to start,

To truly put an end to procrastination, you need a personal impetus. There has to be something deep inside of you that you want to attain, and NLP is a great step in not only discovering that spark but acting on it as well.

A majority of procrastinators would assert that they are prompt and on time with fulfilling required duties. In those cases, facing denial is the first step to becoming the ideal you.

And remember: if you are seriously planning on using NLP to aid in this personal flaw, don't procrastinate. Gather the information you need and get started at your earliest convenience.

NLP and the Law of Attraction

A generally unknown principle known as the law of attraction is just like the law of gravity and force in that, given a formula, you can use it to calculate the outcome of numerous events.

The law of attraction claims that positive thinking spawns positive events and negative thinking spawns negative events. If you have no desire to achieve a goal, reaching it will be much harder for you, even if you possess natural talents.

The law of attraction also works as a makeshift law of energy. Energy fluctuates depending on your state of mind. Being a beautiful person is not enough to make a person feel attractive; rather, believing that one is beautiful is what leads to that sensation of attractiveness.

Likewise, if you have the mindset of a wealthy person, it will become much easier for you to accrue riches.

Similarly, if you think of yourself as nothing more than a middle class citizen, chances are you will have nowhere to go but down.

Positive and Negative Energy

Negative feelings can be transformed into positive ones by having a degree of belief in the plausibility of the change, a vision of the future, and enough passion to make that change.

Whether your energy is positive and negative, it depends on the combination of your beliefs and your actions.

Modifying your beliefs, vision, and passion to match your goals leads to happiness.

Believing You Can Succeed

People are born with a standard set of beliefs that gradually changes depending on their genetics and their environment.

Those beliefs also change as people develop new skills and try out new things in life. Finding and following role models is a method through which current beliefs can be strengthened. When you spend time with people who share similar thoughts as you, it reinforces the idea that your beliefs are right for you. Some beliefs are actually formed because of a role model.

The Neuro Linguistic Program is designed to give you full control over your emotional output. If you need a self-confidence amidst a terrible and sudden turn of events, NLP functions to give you the tools necessary to keep a healthy mindset during the situation.

If neuro-linguistic programming can't get you to alter your feelings and emotions, it should be able to motivate you to work harder towards that end.

Neuro-linguistic programming is like a state of mind - no, more like a lifestyle – where you experience positive changes because you are taking forward steps towards your goals. If you are the let the must-detested element of fear intrude on your hopes and aspirations, you might as well stop dreaming.

Mild fear is natural and may stimulate some people, but in excess, it only serves to damped your progress towards the better you. Negative attraction does exist, and those who experience it tend to believe that they can't do anything. So long as you have the proper mindset, you can accomplish anything.

"Putting yourself in different shoes" is a technique heavily employed by neuro-linguistic programming.

This method can be used to exchange negative attraction for a positive one, thus allowing you to perform better in areas where you might have felt uncomfortable before.

You must learn to view your surroundings in a new light and transform what is mundane into an exciting and exhilarating experience. Attitude, behavior, and belief contribute more to success than many are aware.

Take the following example. Ideally, you would like to win at a particular event. However, during the course of that endeavor, several hardships that impede progress fall upon you.

Each time one of these tragic events befalls you, you cringe and shrivel back into your shell thinking "I won't be able to succeed." Someone with positive attraction wouldn't think that, but something along the lines of "I can learn from this hardship and use that knowledge to either avoid it or help me recover from it faster in the future."

Hardships will occur in every area in your life, but if you are able to take them in stride, even trauma can serve as a step towards your goal.

The neuro-linguistic programming method is becoming a much talked about and appreciated field. Many professionals are starting to legitimize its effectiveness and its realness.

It is one of the few practices that realistically relates behavior, belief, and emotions in such a way that change can be manually applied. With numerous benefits and few side-effects, it's undisputed that NLP is one of the best methods to improve your outlook on life and make a better living for yourself.

It teaches you how to be motivated; it teaches you how to eliminate stress; it teaches you how to be the person and live the life you've always wanted through a very powerful attraction.

NLP and Wallowing in Wealth

To survive in this world, it is required that one have a source of income. Most of us aspire to have a very large one. Being wealthy is an age-old dream that dates back to the age of kings where those with wealth were in control.

That idea remains true today and is very tempting. However, a big misconception is that all wealth takes the form of coin and elaborate possessions. Thus, you'd be a liar to say you didn't seek wealth in some form.

True wealth is anything that can bring a person satisfaction and contentment.

As you might have already imagined, NLP serves as one of the methods capable of generating wealth for you.

Always remember that becoming wealthy typically requires you to develop several skills that NLP is also compatible with. Some of those skills include communication and confidence.

Because prerequisites of gaining wealth with NLP are other areas in which NLP is effective, choosing to use it to increase your income is something of a bonus deal.

The mindset that you develop during the course of learning how you can become a wealthier individual will seep into all other areas of your live, making everything else easier and more profitable. Now that the procedure has been made transparent to you, here are the proper steps:

• Firstly, you must use NLP to gain self-confidence. No venture into the world of business will be successful if you're not confident that you can succeed in your endeavors and that you offer or participate in a service that you believe you can perform well in.

Confidence is simply an essential part of being alive and making progress in life. If gaining access to the riches you have always dreamed of is your foremost dream, you must be confident enough to believe you can do it and have enough self-esteem to turn away anyone who tells you otherwise.

NLP training is the best way to reach both of those goals. In the case of business endeavors, self-confidence gives you everything you need to be on equal footing with people of higher rank than you.

When they see you not scared of them, talking with them as if you are equals, those people will eventually come to respect you.

• After acquiring the qualities outlined in the previous step, it is time to put your abilities to the test in learning how to better communicate with others.

Every business is a system of communications whether it be between employees and their employers, employees and other employees, or employees and customers.

If there is no communication, the business is destined to fail. Board meetings and other business-related matters also become easier to engage in and get a good deal out of.

This is the most important part of moving into a corporate occupation. Learn the tricks of the trade and the lingo to effectively communicate.

Part of succeeding in the business world is giving off the air that you are professional, even if you aren't. There are numerous online sources that will provide you with help getting your first foot in the water.

Many people who venture into the corporate world often sell so much of their life to the endeavor that they forget about the little things. Taking breaks, seeing friends, and relaxing are all second to getting out and making more money.

However, as a living, breathing human being, you are entitled to those things which bring you happiness. It is healthy to occasionally reward yourself for hard work.

Spending time with family and friends, spending a quiet night by yourself, or engaging in any leisure activity can all help to relieve work-related stress.

If you find that NLP has given you the extra edge you needed to live a prosperous life, don't keep the pleasure for yourself.

During the time that you spend with friends and family, let them in on the secrets that paved the road towards your financial growth.

When you share NLP with others and they begin to make the same progress that you have, not only will you be helping them, but you'll be helping yourself.

Maybe they'll have some NLP stories for you that will come in handy in the future; and you can be sure that your grateful friends will repay you for the new lifestyle you have introduced them to. This repayment can come in many forms, so be on the lookout for it.

NLP and Sending Social Phobia to Perish

Social phobia is a disorder that is characterized by irrational fear of social situations. Recognize that social phobia disorder is not something experienced by everyone. Shyness is something that is typical of everyone; only when that shyness is exaggerated and interferes with normal functioning can it be classified as a phobia.

NLP can be used to overcome both forms. A social phobia can be easily recognized by an anxiety response by an individual placed in a social situation, particularly one where humiliation is possible.

Whether or not fear is unreasonable is also subjective to an extent. If you are sitting in a large crowd of five hundred at a magic show and the magician singles you out from the back to come on stage and assist him with his next feat, it wouldn't be unnatural for you to experience a large amount of fear or apprehension.

Another symptom that can be difficult to identify as abnormal or not is hypersensitivity to criticism.

Some people are naturally very sensitive, so that should definitely be taken into account when making a diagnosis. Because these people fear socializing, asserting themselves in social situations is something you shouldn't expect in the least. And if someone suffering from social phobia disorder is under attack by the bully, not only should you expect to see them quiver in fear, but completely draw away from the situation in a frenzy.

Having seen over forty years of growth, NLP has been optimized for solving the aforementioned problem: alleviating negative mindsets and help you to develop into a healthy person.

Now we will make urgent haste into a discourse centered around; how to use neuro-linguistic programming to eliminate social phobia.

Below are the many ways in which you can use NLP to help you overcome your debilitating disorder:

• Emotional Coherence Systems – this technique helps you by increasing motivation, stabilizing emotions, and building interpersonal bonds.

• Reflective Symmetry – making positive comparisons between yourself and a healthy individual or attempting to follow to mold that another has cast.

• Cognitive Dispersal and Realignment – changing the way you think to resemble the way another thinks or mentally transposing yourself into the life of someone else, real or imaginary.

• Psychological Management – this includes vast system of mental operations meant to modify an individual's physiology

• Reimagining – altering the circumstances of an event so that you may get a better perspective on it.

• Translateralism – the process of changing an unconditioned negative behavior into a positive conditioned one through step-by-step alteration of the original behavior.

We have now briefly covered the basic methods of the neuro-linguistic program that may be of assistance in helping you to overcome any social phobias you may have. Most certainly, there are more advanced techniques out there, techniques that may require separate books themselves!

NLP is just so vast and complex that everything cannot be touched upon in an introductory text. However, it shouldn't do any harm to go over a few of those advanced techniques there in case you want to do some additional digging around for them.

1. Semi-Submissive Subjection – this super-advanced method involves transferring both your body and mind to a higher level of logical comprehension and analytical ability, allowing you to better process what is going on in your life and how to promote change

2. Multi-Derivative Consciousness – this method connects your lower states of thought to your higher ones, allowing you to counsel yourself. It can also be used to help you interact with people who may not know how to socialize with your lower states.

3. Language Patterns – memorizing common patterns in your native language that are frequently used (expressions, word/letter combinations, body gestures, etc.).

4. Refiguration – mentally processing an image of yourself that is substantially better and far more desirable than who you really are. The desire to fulfill that

reality will be enough to push you beyond the edge of your limits to develop new behaviors.

These powerful, advanced techniques should only be attempted after you have made yourself comfortable with the basic ones.

The higher you progress, the more NLP will be able to help you overcome your social anxiety. If you need any assistance with the advanced techniques, professionals in the field of NLP are available to give you a hand.

NLP and Creating Confidence

Without self-confidence, there is absolutely nothing that you would be able to accomplish – you'd be too wary of failure. How highly you regard yourself in terms of your ability, the more capable you will be of accomplishing the tasks that need to be completed.

Every successful person is confident that they have what it takes to do the things they do. Even if you don't aspire to be the next Steve Jobs, your future still requires that you have a base of self-confidence to support your dreams.

Unfortunately, there are many variables that affect self-confidence, many of which are completely out of our control. However, that does not mean that these forces cannot be counteracted. You're going to learn how using NLP.

Sometimes people try to rationalize not being confident by pointing out traits of confident people that they dislike.

For example, there is a connection between confidence and cockiness, unconfident people often labeling self-confidence as its counterpart. This is not at all true in every situation.

Others think that if you're overly confident and all of your plans end up failing, they'll be faced with painful humiliation; their goal is to avoid that humiliation by being humble or by having no self-confidence. Like every other condition in this book, low self-confidence can be improved by NLP.

The first step is something we have done multiple times in the past: finding a solid reason for deciding that it's time to transform into a newer, more confident person.

Also, at this time, you will want to identify any underlying irrational thinking that may be trapping you in a cycle of low self-confidence. One of the most common problems with teenagers and divorced adults is a fear of rejection.

This fear only increases as more rejections are experienced, but having confidence in your decisions and who you are as a person can help you to overcome these. Maybe you can find a way to transform that lingering fear of rejection into pleasure, a sort of adrenaline to help you appear more confident.

Now it's time for us to discuss what the multiple neuro-linguistic techniques at your disposal do:

• Imagine yourself in a world of excess, excess only possible because you were able to increase your confidence. Visualize the people you associate with, the possessions you own, and the exotic locales you have visited.

What you imaging doesn't necessarily have to be realistic; it only needs serve as an inspiration for you to take the first step on the journey to redefining who you are. Think of the many experiences that you have been blessed with due to this new self-confidence.

This is one of the most important steps. Synthesize your future happiness in your mind until you have the drive to move on with the plan.

• The next step is equally important. When you have decided what kind of person you want to be, change back to imagining yourself the way you are now.

Measure how much joy and contentment was lost when you switched between the two scenarios. When you come to realize the monumental difference between the two, you will finally see that it's time to make a big change in your life.

With those two objectives complete, you have created cognitive dissonance by acknowledging the rift between what you are and what you know you could be.

At this point, you should be realizing the importance of self-confidence and the role that it plays in your life. The way you see yourself will make a change for the better as you begin to steer towards the new path you have invisioned for yourself. If, while you are working to attain that new life experience, you do so with the mindset of the person you hope to eventually become, the process will be that much easier for you because you won't have to build up to having that state of mind anymore.

This may be difficult because you have yet to become confident. To help you along the way, create a list of your best qualities physical, mental, and emotional. These are the things you should focus on instead of the negative.

Read, review the list every day, and modify it when appropriate. Until you truly begin to have faith in the listed qualities, do not stop reading the list.

As you become confident in traits, remove them from the list; as you discover new, good things about yourself, add them to the list.

As you come to respect yourself for those qualities, your self-confidence will gradually increase.

It's only normal that people seek to prevent as much pain in their lives as possible. However, as the saying goes, pleasure wouldn't be possible without pain. Besides, once we have been faced with hardship, it pushes us to prevail in the future.

If you are unable to do that, then the neuro-linguistic programming techniques might be the only way for you to claim a life worth living.

Just think of all the great things you could have if only you were more confident. The world is under your feet.

Combining NLP with Modeling Techniques

Those who have trained in NLP serve as excellent models for spreading the knowledge of how critically important communication is, and how effective the programming method is in sharpening that area to help you overcome a plethora of roadblocks you may be facing in your life.

We can only overcome our issues if we have full confidence that it is possible. As you have probably experienced from reading this book and practicing the techniques contained within, NLP training is a widely overlooked solution for those who may not know how to muster enough confidence to live comfortable lives or chase their dreams.

Now that you have come to reach those many revelations, there is one final step before you can truly call yourself a master of the art of NLP. That last objective is to become a role model for others to follow so that neuro-linguistic programming's benefits can spread as far as possible.

The term "modeling techniques" doesn't only mean setting an example for other people to follow. It also refers to the way you simultaneously learn and apply your knowledge to the situations that arise in the future.

In essence, you are modeling your future based on the principles of NLP. Of course, applying NLP to your life does involve sharing the knowledge with others, and when you give them the motivation they need to succeed, it will also increase your confidence in a self-fulfilling prophecy of success.

Think about this concept for a moment. The teachings of the neuro-linguistic program can only be spread when people make the choice to follow them through to the end.

Everyone who reaches the end of their NLP training will be enticed to spread their knowledge either through the doctrine of the program or by their own free will. Either way, their application of modeling techniques will cause them to share the story with people who they know, thus allowing the ideas of neuro-linguistic programming to spread further. Imagine how many lives you've indirectly changed?

This process of learning will continue indefinitely.

That aside, there are several more ways your life can be enriched by practicing modeling techniques, outlined as follows:

• Foremost, you needn't be told this first part; as you venture out into the world, you should come to the revelation on your own that as you share what you've learned with others, it reinforces your beliefs, making you even more confident. This will keep you pushing forward to accomplish more of your goals and to do it increasingly more efficiently. All aspects of your life with drastically improve.

• Second, your new outlook on life gives you the potential to change the way you perceive you in the case you begin to amass a publicized amount of extravagance. Most middle and lower class citizens are wrongly under the assumption that wealthy individuals are naturally snobby and rude money-grubbers with no concerns for the lower classes. Your ability to utilize NLP in conjunction with modeling techniques can cause alterations to those faulty beliefs by presenting yourself to the public is as bright a light as humanly possible. Public speaking is a great way to get this message out. After all of the NLP training you have been doing, effectively communicating with potentially hostile crowds should be no problem for you. If they are, all you need to do is use NLP techniques to engrain in yourself the patience you need to overcome their oppression.

• Lastly, your proficiency in advanced programming techniques will open up to you the door to inner peace. Very similar to meditation, it allows you to instantly enter yourself into a state of zen so that you may recuperate from the struggles of the day and clear your mind of any doubts you may have. This specialized form of concentration also gives you the ability to command absolute respect from those who realize the great life that you have finally achieved.

Everyone can find a way to benefit from the spread of information related to neuro-linguistic programming. The hidden realities of life reveal themselves to both parties.

The benefits of using NLP in personal and professional areas of life soon become completely clear.

Combining Modeling Techniques with Communication

Of all of the goals you can accomplish through learning to better communicate, convincing other of the legitimacy of your beliefs is the hardest.

The process of using NLP to enhance your communication skills really all leads up to this point: the moment when you use those skills to truly make a difference in the world.

You will be able to weave an intricate, emotional tale about how neuro-linguistic programming was able to shape your life for the better.

You may not realize until now that we've never talked explicitly about what techniques you can use to directly benefit your ability to clearly communicate with others. So we will begin to examine that here.

• The more experience you have in communicating with other people, the more prepared you will be to give an incredible performance in social situation. This can mean you will be more capable of getting other people to understand just how much NLP can benefit them throughout their lives. When people are confused, perhaps in academics, you will have no problem helping to explain concepts to them in a way that they can understand. And if people don't quite understand your personal goals and motivations, you will easily be able to clear up any misunderstandings they may have.

• If you don't think yourself to be an effective communicator, NLP targets the most important skill in aiding in enhanced communication: confidence. Though a big part of effectively relaying your thoughts and ideas is having a firm grasp on the concepts you wish to represent, the biggest part is having confidence in what you're saying.

• Most importantly, NLP assists people in developing more resilient, rigid mindsets. If you have training in NLP and someone tries to put you down, you will have the mental fortitude to be able to negate that negative comment and focus only on the positive aspects of yourself.

These, and many more, are some of the near infinite possibilities once you decide to embrace NLP.

However, don't think that this is a miracle cure to your problems. The effectiveness of these techniques is directly related to how much you truly want to reshape the way you live your life.

Simply put, if there are aspects of NLP that you do not agree with, it will be substantially more difficult for you to use them as tools for your growth. Conversely, the more you let the knowledge become part of who you are, the fewer hardships you will face on the road to fulfilling your dreams. Going into NLP with the wrong mindset can have adverse effects.

Consequently, you must make an assessment of yourself beforehand. Without proper motivation for undergoing the training, you may find yourself in a worse situation than when you started.

NLP should not be used for selfish reasons. It's not a tool for the rich to become even more so or for the jocks to score even more girls. It's a methodology through which those who may not have the greatest skill set gain the confidence they need to be successful. Wave away the you of the past so that you can embrace the invigorated, new you who has experienced all of the benefits that NLP has to offer.

Final Words

Most people who lack confidence are well aware of that fact. They'd like to be more outspoken but simply can't.

They don't know how to train themselves to have faith or believe that their opinions have a hefty value. This doesn't mean that they try at every turn, struggling through internal dialogues, the seed of doubt always sprouting into a colossal forest of fear, overshadowing what little courage sits pent up within them.

If you are one of those people, this is the perfect opportunity for you. There is a wide range of obscure teachings built specifically for you.

Most people regard them as gimmicks, but these have the power to change your entire life if you're willing to give them the chance.

Enclosed within the pages of this book, you'll find basic information regarding NLP, or neuro-linguistic programming, an advanced self-help technique that's sure to pick you up from the slumps of self-pity into the realm of confidence and achievement.

Printed in Great Britain
by Amazon.co.uk, Ltd.,
Marston Gate.